ESSEX SPAS

AND
MINERAL WATERS

Ronald and Ann Cowell

IAN HENRY PUBLICATIONS

ISBN 0 86025 519 0

The cover picture
is an engraving, dated 1882,
of Dovercourt, with the Spa
in the foreground

Published by
Ian Henry Publications, Ltd.
20 Park Drive, Romford, Essex RM1 4LH
and printed by
ColourBooks, Ltd.
Dublin, 13, Ireland

FIRST THOUGHTS

In the eighteenth century bottles of mineral water from Essex were sold in London and travelled abroad with the English as they colonised the world. In the nineteenth century a spa was set up in Essex where you could take the waters and attend elegant assemblies. It had ambitions to rival Bath and Tunbridge Wells but never became nationally famous and faded into obscurity. In the twentieth century another bottled water from Essex became a national sensation, only to disappear a few years later amongst rumours of pollution. As we enter the twenty-first century there is Essex spring water on the international market taken from a spring probably used by the Romans.

One of the vital necessities for the site of a settlement is a clean, reliable source of water. In Essex several Iron Age settlements have been found near springs such as at Chimneys Farm, Witham, and at Wickham Bishops. Roman remains have been found near springs and wells in Colchester.

Probably in later times, the Church declared that local springs should be sanctified and they became "Holy Wells". Those near churches took on the name of the saint to which the church was dedicated. Later still these springs were alleged to have curative properties and people began to use the waters to rid themselves of digestive and skin disorders.

Written evidence for the use of the wells of Essex appeared in a book by Dr Benjamin Allen in 1699 in which he writes about the chalybeate water of Wanstead, Witham, South Weald, Upminster, Great Leighs, Felsted, Marks Hall, Woodham Ferrers and Colchester.

'Pilgrims' visited South Weald, as well as patients from a leper hospital near Brentwood who thought the water would cure them. It was thought that the Colchester spring was probably discovered and used by native settlers and Romans in the early Roman occupation of Essex. There are Roman remains near the well at Felsted.

In the eighteenth century several more springs were added to the list of those already used and water from the two at West Tilbury was bottled and sold in London. Others, such as those at Havering, Chigwell Row, Hornchurch, Plaistow and Ilford, were also used as local water supplies as well as having 'curative' properties. The well at Hornchurch was thought to be useful in curing eye complaints and infections. Woodford Wells was widely visited by Londoners, as it was only a horse ride from the city. Most of these wells fell into disuse as the villages became towns and suburbs of Greater London. They became 'lost' beneath houses and industrial development. Old maps show where these waters were to be found, but often the only evidence of their whereabouts are plaques, such as that of St Chad's Well in Billet Road, Chadwell Heath, and Havering Well at Roneo Corner.

In the nineteenth century two spas were developed. Hockley had a sumptuous building made to rival that at Cheltenham or Tunbridge Wells, but its stardom was short lived, five years at the most. Dovercourt was built and opened in 1854, at the same time as the railway reached the ferry terminal at Harwich. This spa was more successful as it survived into the twentieth century until its demise at the outbreak of the Great War in 1914, when the buildings were taken over by the army.

At OWEN's Original Mineral-Water Warehouſe,

(Late EYRES's) between the Temple Gates, Fleet Street,

(Eſtabliſhed in its reputation near *fifty years*, by the recommendation of the moſt *eminent Phyſicians*)
Are ſold, wholeſale or retale (*for ready money only*) all ſorts of MINERAL WATERS, now in
uſe, or preſcribed by the *Faculty*, in their utmoſt perfection, and at the following Prices:

	l. s. d.			l. s. d.
SEltzer water, in large ſtone bottles at	1 1 0	Cheltenham water — at	0 10 0
German Spa water, filled at the Penbon Spring, in large flaſks	0 14 0	Bath water —	0 9 0
		Scarborough water —	0 9 0
The ſame, in ſmall flaſks	0 10 0	Briſtol hot well water, from *Smith* and *Wodall*	0 7 0
Pyrmont water, in three-pint bottles	1 1 0		
Bourn water, in large ſtone bottles	0 18 0	Jeſſop's well, or Stoke water —	0 7 0
Harrogate Spa water —	0 12 0	Acton, and Dog and Duck waters —	0 6 0
Nevil Holt water, from Dr. *Short*	0 12 0	Tar water, made agreeable to Bp. *Barkley's* directions	0 6 0
Wiltſhire Holt water —	0 12 0		
Tilbury alterative water, from the old well	0 10 0	Sea water, in its utmoſt purity, taken up ſeveral leagues at ſea	0 6 0
Malvern —	0 12 0		
Shadwell water —	0 12 0		

Scarborough ſalts, 2s. 6d. per ounce.   Cheltenham ſalts, 2s. per ounce.   Acton ſalts, 6d. per ounce.

N. B. The foreign waters are taken up at ſuch times only, when they are in full vigour, and approved by the phyſicians both of *Pyrmont* and *Spa*, as will more fully appear by ſeveral certificates under their hands and ſeals.

The waters of *Bru* being notoriouſly ſold at a low price, for the true *Penbon water of Spa*, to the great diſappointment of the phyſicians and their patients; (as appears by the following certificate, the original of which is in my poſſeſſion) in order to prevent impoſitions (*ſo dangerous to health*) as much as lies in my power, I preſume to deſire the favour of thoſe who are ſo kind as to honour me with their commands, to give ſtrict orders, that the meſſenger do always bring back one of theſe printed bills, with a receipt ſigned by their moſt obedient ſervant,

W. OWEN.

We do prefer the waters of the *Penbon Spring in Spa to any of the mineral waters lay or near the quality of Liege*, particularly to the waters of *Bru*, which waters have been notoriouſly impoſed on the public for the true *Penbon* water, to our and our patients diſappointment.

September, 1733.

Ham Skene,	N. Broxholme,	Tho. Weſt,	Tho. Pellet,
John Shadwell,	R. Mead,	J. Burton,	Alexander Stuart,
Jo. Hervey,	Tamred Robinſon,	John Hollings,	M. Lee.

Note. *Bath, Briſtol, Sea*, and ſeveral of the above waters, come conſtantly freſh every week, by land carriage.

Mr *Dickinſon* London, 1769
Bought of W. OWEN, at his Mineral Water Warehouſe, in Fleetſtreet,

18 — 2 Doz Briſtol — — — 0 . 14 . 0

baſket — — £0 . 1 . 0

£0 . 15 . 0

Rec'd Contents

Wm Owen

Owen's Original Mineral-Water Warehouse price list, including Tilbury, Bath
and Malvern waters

By permission of the Guildhall Library, Corporation of London

Since the closure of Dovercourt in 1919, Essex mineral water seemed to have lost its earlier popularity, although water from the springs at Vange was bottled and sold. An attractive rotunda was built for people to visit and it still stands in Langdon Hills Country Park. The two companies that sold the water stopped in 1926 when the water became contaminated.

Vange Water Company was the last available bottled water until Hockley water was marketed in the 1980s and then in 1997 when the Spring Clear concern became a business. This latter operation is in an apple orchard near Wickham Bishops. This water is advertised as 'Our own natural spring that has been a pure water source for centuries' and is 'a low calorie drink that is enjoyed by millions'. The company has joined in the current fashion for drinking bottled water and seems to be a successful business.

The name of Miller Christy will keep cropping up throughout the following pages. In 1910 he published a survey of all the springs and wells, of which he could find documentary evidence and which were considered by the local people to produce medicinal waters. His book has been our inspiration and we are covering all the springs which have been commercially exploited and some of the more important of the remainder, plus some others which have been discovered since Mr Christy's book was published.

We have used the words springs and wells interchangeably, but in actual fact all the sites started as natural springs, and wells were often dug on the location in order to obtain waters in greater quantities.

WHAT IS A MINERAL WATER?

What makes a spring water a mineral water? At the time Miller Christy was researching in the early years of the twentieth century, a mineral water was one containing a higher than normal concentration of minerals. Nowadays any natural spring water would be described as a mineral water. But what makes it a medicinal water? The short answer is a water with a very high salt mineral content and in addition it should contain magnesium or iron salts. Medicinal waters can be divided into three kinds.

Firstly, there are the sulphur waters, which contain sulphur compounds and are known by their bad eggs smell of hydrogen sulphide. They are claimed to be good for skin complaints and for soothing the stomach. These waters are not found in Essex, probably the most famous example being at Harrogate where you can still drink them. They are an acquired taste!

Secondly, there are chalybeate waters containing iron and which are often reddish in colour from the formation of ferric oxide (rust) when they are exposed to air. Witham and Dovercourt were both claimed to be chalybeate wells, but we have no analytical figures for Witham to support this claim, as the site was lost before Miller Christy travelled around Essex taking his samples.

Thirdly, there are saline waters, with high concentrations of salts, mainly sulphates and chlorides of magnesium and sodium. Magnesium sulphate is commonly known as Epsom Salts as it was the main constituent of the water from the mineral springs at Epsom, famous in the seventeenth and eighteenth centuries.

MINERAL WATERS.

JOHN ELLISON,

BEGS Leave to acquaint the Nobility, and Public in general, That on the First of *July*, 1778, he purchased the Lease of Mr. DAVIS's MINERAL WATER WARE-HOUSE, next the *St. Alban's Tavern*, in *St. Alban's-Street*, PALL-MALL; where he hopes for a Continuance of their Favours. On the Twentieth of the same Month he purchased the Lease of that excellent MINERAL WATER, known by the Name of JESSOP's WELL, or STOKE MINERAL WATER, situate on *Stoke Common*, near *Clermont*, *Surry*, the Property of the said Mr. DAVIS.——As other spurious Waters have been imposed on the Public, for that of the genuine Spring, to prevent such Imposition in future, all Bottles are sealed at the Well, and at my Warehouses, with a *Chevron*, between three Eagles Heads erased; round the Seal, *Jessop's Well Water*, *John Ellison*, *Proprietor*.——Those who wish to drink *Jessop Well Water* in its greatest Perfection, are desired to send to ELLISON's MINERAL WATER WAREHOUSE, in *St. Alban's-Street*, PALL-MALL, or to his Warehouse at No. 33, near *Red-Lion Street*, WHITE-CHAPEL, where it comes constantly fresh every Week, and to no other Place in *London*.

	Per Dozen.			Per Dozen.
Bath and Scarborough Water, —	0 9 0	Harrogate Spa Water, — —	0 12 0
Bristol Hot-well Water, — —	0 8 0	Tilbury Alterative Water, —	0 10 0
Jessop's Well or Stoke Water, —	0 8 0	Nevil Holt Water, — —	0 12 0
Seltzer Water, large Stone Bottles,	1 1 0	Wiltshire Holt Water, —	0 12 0
Pyrmont Water, in three Pint ditto,	1 4 0	Sea and Tar Water, —	0 6 0
German Spa Water, large Flasks,	0 18 0	Malvern Water, —	0 12 0
The same in small Flasks, —	0 12 0	Scarborough Salts, per Oz. —	0 1 6
Cheltenham Water, — —	0 12 0	Cheltenham Salts, per Oz. —	0 1 0

Bought of John Ellison, in St. Alban's-Street, Pall-Mall.

John Ellison's Mineral Waters price list, including Tilbury, Harrogate and Cheltenham waters

By permission of the Guildhall Library, Corporation of London

Waters of this type are known mainly for their purgative effects. All the remaining Essex wells are of this type, although only four, South Weald, Upminster, Hockley and Vange, have high enough concentrations of salts to be considered medicinal waters. The water at Hockley, in fact, seems to have changed over the years so that, whilst Mr Christy considered it to be medicinal water, by the 1980s the salt content had fallen considerably and it was sold as table water. But perhaps the value of the waters wasn't in what they contained.

Before the middle of the nineteenth century towns did not have good water supplies and the mineral springs provided a source of fresh pure liquid. The drinking of large quantities of mineral waters was recommended in the eighteenth and nineteenth centuries. At the spas, as well as drinking the water, visitors would normally enjoy the attendance of a physician who would recommend a healthy life-style including exercise and fresh air. At many spas baths and other water treatments could be taken. Baths may have been available at Witham and Hockley, but there is no direct evidence and it is unlikely that they were. In addition visitors could enjoy the company of other patients in what was a kind of holiday atmosphere. And finally there was faith. Until fairly modern times there was little that doctors could do to cure illnesses and recommending spa treatment gave an impression of positive action. A combination of all these regimes could well have a curative effect.

THE WATERS OF WEST TILBURY

West Tilbury Hall is on top of a grassy hill above the marsh formed by the River Thames. It was here in 1724 that Mr Kellaway sank a well to provide water for his farm. He said that he dug the well to use as a water supply for his house. It was near other springs and at least 50 feet above the marshy ground at the bottom of the hill and was about 12 feet deep. There was a band of sand 30 feet deep at 13 feet from the surface so that the water was filtered by the sand and was clear and pure at the outlet. The well was about 40 feet away from the house.

It was in 1727 that Kellaway discovered the medicinal properties of his well when he was troubled with gout and a cold. While visiting his farm at Tilbury he was advised to drink the water and soon regained his health. He was fond of drinking milk at the farm, but complained that it had what he described as a purging effect on him. He found that if he drank a glass of water before taking the milk he didn't have any more problems.

Later, in 1737, he suffered a bout of diarrhoea that was alleviated by the water from his well mixed with wine. He was so impressed that he ordered his farm manager to recommend drinking the water to any of his workers who were troubled by the said 'distemper' or 'looseness', as he described it.

He even found that his calves benefited from drinking spring-water when they were sick. They were normally treated with a remedy made from boiling oak bark in water. Kellaway's first approaches to the medical profession, or The Faculty as it was known, were not well received and he was told that there were more mineral waters already in use than were necessary. So for a while the water was distributed free to his friends and acquaintances in London and Tilbury.

The well came to the attention of Dr John Andree (1699-1785), later to become the first physician of the London Hospital, who wrote a pamphlet extolling the virtues of the Tilbury water. The pamphlet was dedicated to Sir Hans Sloane, Physician to the King and President of the Royal Society. It relates the many conditions which the water was said to cure including, diarrhoea, dysentery and bleeding of piles. It relieved the gravel and stone, asthma, gout, diseases of the bowels and scorbutic ailments. Its main use appeared to be for the treatment of common ailments such as scurvy, 'bloody fluxes' and diarrhoea that in those days of little personal hygiene were rife in most households.

Dr Andree used the water for treating his patients, as also did the more famous Sir Hans Sloane, and its fame spread. During the years from 1737 to 1783 Andree wrote four editions of his pamphlet praising and reporting on the efficacy of Tilbury water.

The water was eventually put on the market at a shilling a bottle with a penny back on the empties, or you could buy it in bulk at ten shillings a dozen. In 1765 it was sold in London at Mr Davis's, purveyor to His Majesty, in St Alban's Street, Pall Mall, and at the Jerusalem Coffee House in Cornhill. It could also be bought in Gravesend, for the shipping market, and in Essex at the well and at Messrs Strupar and Haffalls, stationers in Chelmsford.

By 1778 John Ellison had come on to the scene. He was described as a druggist and proprietor of mineral water at his warehouses in Whitechapel and

Pall Mall having purchased the lease of the latter from Mr Davis. He was advertising both Tilbury Water and Jessop Water listing a number of places in London where they could have been bought and mentioning an export business to the East and West Indies. His advertisement concluded with the following statement,

"The proprietor, being desirous that no part of the community should be deprived of these Waters, respectfully acquaints the clergy, Gentlemen of The Faculty, and Ladies and Gentlemen who wish to serve their poor neighbours, that by sending letters, with proper recommendation to John Ellison at his Mineral Water Warehouse shall receive Jessop and Tilbury waters gratis." [Jessop Water came from Jessop's Well at Stoke Common, near Claremont in Surrey].

The following year John Ellison became the proprietor of the Tilbury well and published the following announcement.

"John Ellison's respectful compliments to the dealers in Mineral Waters, begs leave to acquaint them ... on the 11th January, 1779, he purchased the lease of that much approved water, called Tilbury Alterative Water, situated at West Tilbury Hall, Essex. The characteristic marks of this water are, its being a soft straw colour, and having an extreme soft, pleasant taste like milk, which circumstances are particularly mentioned by Dr Andree, Dr Rutty, Dr Munro and other eminent physicians. An excellent Treatise written by Dr Andree on the discovery and virtues of this water, may be had gratis of the proprietor. Those who intend selling these waters, are desired to send their address to the proprietor, John Ellison, at his Mineral Water Warehouse, in St Alban's Street, Pall Mall, or to his warehouse, near

TILBURY WATER.

SIR,

I READILY comply with your requeſt, in hopes that your intended publication of my caſe may be uſeful to all that are afflicted as I have been.

From my fifty-ſixth to my fifty-eighth year, I was frequently attacked with torment-ing pains in my back and loins, ſhooting downwards, and attended with ſickneſs at my ſtomach and loſs of appetite. My water came reddiſh in very ſmall quantity, with great difficulty and intolerable pain. It was frequently mixt with tough ſlime, and at other times with clotted blood, and great quantities of gravel. At the ſame time my body was ſwelled to an extraordinary ſize, and I was continually troubled with wind and pain in my bowels. During many months theſe diſorders were imputed to gravel in the kidney and bladder, and I took vaſt quantities of medicine without any relief. At laſt the late Dr. HOOPER, of St. *Martin's-lane*, adviſed me to try TILBURY WATER, which I had from the MINERAL WATER WAREHOUSE, in St. *Alban's-ſtreet*. In a few days after, I began to drink it at the rate of a bottle a day; my water came in due quantity, the pains ceaſed, the ſwelling in my body and bowels ſubſided, and the gravel paſſed off eaſily.

From this period which was in my fifty-eighth year, to the eighty-ſecond, I have at times been alarmed with ſome ſlight returns of the ſame diſorder, from which I was as often relieved ſo ſoon as I had recourſe to the TILBURY WATER.

In the ſeventy-ſecond or ſeventy-third year of my age, painful ſores broke out on the ſkin under my breaſts, and lower down, which dried up and diſappeared, on my taking the TILBURY WATER. Theſe, which were called ſcorbutic, frequently returned during ten years, and were as often ſpeedily healed by the uſe of the ſame water. About eight months ago, in my eighty-ſecond year, an eruption appeared on many parts of my body and limbs, which made the ſkin hard and ſcaly; for this I drank the water with the uſual ſucceſs, and now I enjoy as good health as any woman at eighty-three can reaſon-ably expect. All that I have related is known to many, if not to all, my neighbours, amongſt whom I have lived on this ſpot above forty years.

I am, S I R, your humble Servant,

No. 11. *Bath-Court, Cold-Bath Fields,*   JANE BROWN.
    Sept. 22, 1783.

———

THE public are reſpectfully requeſted to obſerve, that the above remarkable cure was performed by the water of *Weſt Tilbury Hall*, which has been found to contain nearly double the quantity of Medicinal Ingredients of any other ſpring of *Tilbury*. To prevent waters of inferior ſtrength being impoſed on the public, Mr. ELLISON's Name, with the words WEST TILBURY HALL, is expreſſed on the bottles.

As Mr. ELLISON does not deſire to with-hold from perſons in narrow circumſtances the benefit of thoſe waters which are his ſole property, they ſhall be ſupplied with *Jeſſop* and *Tilbury* water *gratis* from the wells or the above warehouſes, on ſending their addreſs.

ALL the MINERAL WATERS with the ESSENCE of AMERICAN SPRUCE and SPRUCE BEER, may be had in the greateſt perfection,

At ELLISON's WAREHOUSES, in *St. Alban's Street, Pall-Mall*; and near *Red Lion Street, Whitechapel.*

John Ellison's advertising leaflet used testimonials to publicise Tilbury Water
By permission of the Essex Record Office

Red Lion Street, Whitechapel, and their names will be inserted in his further advertisements."

A Mr Lamb who sold water from Bath, Bristol, Cheltenham, Harrogate and Scarborough also included Tilbury Water amongst his stock thus giving high recommendation for it, and showing that it was highly regarded at that time.

Not only did Ellison sell water from his warehouses but also he was a very enterprising vendor who also sold it from a horse drawn cart, which ran three times a week between his two warehouses in London. Orders could be sent in advance to the Three Kings in Bloomsbury and the King's Head in Oxford Street for immediate delivery.

But then a rival water appeared advertising its virtues. It was described as 'GENUINE TILBURY ALTERATIVE WATER from the Original Spring'. It purported to cure all loosenesses, the bloody flux, and to be very useful in relieving piles and other bleedings. It could be used as an excellent restorative for anyone with internal decay or wasting weaknesses, either male or female. The advertising hype goes on to extol more virtues and its advertiser tells people how best to serve it. Apparently it mixed well with arrack, rum, brandy, wine or milk and if customers wanted recommendations they could consult Dr Rutty's Treatise on mineral waters. The late Dr [Peter] Shaw [1694-17631], physician to His late Majesty, and several prominent physicians of the time had particularly recommended it. This water was sold by appointment at Mr Owen's water warehouse, Temple Bar, at Mr Lamb's, purveyor to His Majesty, in New Bond Street, Mr Andrew's wine vaults, Saville Row, at ten shillings per dozen bottles and five shillings per half dozen. The bottles were

A remarkable Instance of the Efficacy of
TILBURY WATER.

MR. ELLISON thinks it incumbent on him to present the following Relation to the Public, knowing that they will make the proper Distinction between Empirical Advertisements, and the authentic Testimonies which he produces of the Effects of Medicines, which NATURE only prepares; and whose Ingredients have been, at Mr. ELLISON's Instance, *not concealed*, but discovered, and published at a great Expence, for the Satisfaction of liberal Practitioners, and the Benefit of Mankind.

A few Weeks ago, an entire Stranger to Mr. ELLISON, a Mr. NASH, Coachmaker, in *Worship-street, Moorfields*, called upon him, to inform him, that Mrs. NASH, his Wife, had received an extraordinary Cure from the TILBURY WATER, which he had prevailed upon her to try, by reading to her the remarkable Case of Mrs. BROWN, of *Cold Bath Fields*, published in the Newspapers of *September*, 1783. He at the same Time expressed a Wish to Mr. ELLISON, that her Case might be made public, for the Benefit of those who labour under the like Disease: In consequence of which, Mr. ELLISON waited on Mrs. NASH, on the 15th Inst. and received the following Account.

Above four Years ago, Mrs. NASH, then in the forty-sixth year of her Age, was attacked with a violent Diarrhœa, accompanied with Vomiting, griping Pains, and extreme Weakness. In a little Time, her Food and Drink passed through unaltered, and from a corpulent Habit, she was reduced to an emaciated and desperate State, having, during several Months, received no permanent Relief from Medicines, which were frequently administred to her. Under these Circumstances, she tried Tilbury Water, and finding Relief in a few Days, persisted in the Use of it for three or four Months, at the Expiration of which, she was completely cured; and now is as healthy and as corpulent as she was before, and is ready to vouch for the Truth of this Relation to any Lady or Gentleman, that will call on her for that Purpose.

As Waters of inferior Strength to that of *West Tilbury Hall*, by which the above Cure was peformed, have been, and now are, imposed on the Public, under the Title of *Tilbury Alterative Water*, and put into Bottles similar to Mr. ELLISON's; to prevent such Impositions in future, Mr. ELLISON's Name, with the Words " WEST TILBURY HALL," is expressed on the Bottles; of which the Public are respectfully desired to take particular Notice.

The above WATER is Sold by the PROPRIETOR,

JOHN ELLISON,

At his MINERAL WATER WAREHOUSES, *St. Alban's Street, Pall Mall*, and near *Red Lion Street, Whitechapel*.

Where SPRUCE BEER, made from the Essence of American Spruce, may be had in the greatest Perfection.

By permission of the Essex Record Office

13

sealed with a dolphin in the middle and the words Tilbury Alterative Water around it so that no one would mistake it for the other Tilbury water. With that fierce kind of coverage no one would dare buy the other water!

The rival water came from a source that rose in a field near West Tilbury Hall but next to the church on the side of the hill. The water issued from a pump in the parsonage house, which has since been demolished but gave it the name of the Rector's well. Chemical analysis showed that the two Tilbury waters were very similar.

Ellison replied to this competition by publishing a fourth edition of Andree's treatise and by issuing leaflets detailing the remarkable cures resulting from drinking the water he sold. One of the leaflets gave details of a testimonial given to him by a Mrs Nash. Apparently Mrs. Nash who was forty-six years old was suffering an attack of what we might call gastroenteritis with all its attendant symptoms, but after she had become very emaciated and worried she tried Tilbury Water and found relief from her illness in a few days and, after drinking it for several months, claimed she was cured and regained her previous good health and girth. The pamphlet goes on to state that the only way customers would know that they were buying Mr Ellison's mineral water was by the words West Tilbury Hall and Mr Ellison's name being impressed on the glass.

The authors have seen two bottle seals, but neither fits the description. One seal bears the inscription 'I. E. West Tilbury Hall' and the other 'Tilbury Alterative Water - Rd. Hunt'. Lieutenant Colonel Richard Hunt was the owner of West Tilbury Hall in 1783.

By this time both waters were known as Tilbury Alterative Water and Ellison and Owen were still advertising extensively, but Ellison seemed to be more interested in his Jessop water at this time. Interest in seawater was growing, although John Ellison tried to counteract this by suggesting that magnesia salts dissolved in his mineral waters would be just as effective. Even so interest in and the use of Tilbury water declined and by the end of the eighteenth century the famous water was no longer as popular as previously.

When Miller Christy wrote in 1910 both wells still existed, although the water was not being extracted or bottled. West Tilbury Hall water came up from beneath the floor of the dairy and Christy was able to sample it. The Rector's Well was in the Church Field on the site of the old rectory near the south-east corner of the hill.

Christy said that the mouth of the well was open and not fenced so it must have been dangerous to men and animals. It was about nineteen feet deep, and had some three feet of water in it. The well was approximately four feet in diameter, but smaller at the top and it was bricked round with small bricks to a depth of about ten feet, below which the sides were apparently of firm sand. The water was very dirty and polluted with animal and vegetable matter and smelled foul.

Nowadays neither well is visible. The Hall has been refurbished and the dairy, having passed through a period of being a kitchen, is now a snooker room. The well was not discovered during the alterations. The Rector's Well has been lost to sight beneath the field. On the other side of the road is a cottage that was thought to have been built for a custodian of that well. This cottage, if it did house the caretaker, is all that remains of the longest lasting mineral water business in Essex.

Some of the bottle seals are in private hands and one of the bottles has been acquired by Thurrock Museum, where you can see an interesting display relating to the Tilbury Water, included in the displays of past industries and businesses in the Grays area.

One of several designs of seals use on bottles of Tilbury Water

By permission of the Thurrock Historical Society

Tilbury Waters were sold in 2 pint bottles identified by glass seals

By permission of Thurrock Museum

WITHAM SPA

Mineral springs near Witham were discovered in the middle of the seventeenth century. Dr Benjamin Allen mentioned them in his book about medicinal waters in 1699. He did not seem very impressed by their curative properties and omitted them from a later edition of the book in 1711.

However, in 1736 Dr James Taverner, a local doctor, decided to revive one of the springs. Taverner was born in Maldon and studied at Clare Hall, Cambridge. He was admitted as an Extra-Licentiate of the College of Physicians in 1731/32 and became a Bachelor of Medicine at Cambridge in 1733. He practised at Sudbury and then in Witham.

Dr Taverner described the town as being neat, but not inferior because of its small size. It was plentifully supplied with fresh food from nearby fishing ports, and meat and vegetables from the countryside were available at the market. The town was situated on the main road from London to the port of Harwich. Stagecoaches and post chaises passed through at regular intervals and the town had plenty of accommodation and entertainment for everyone. So the stage was set for Taverner's enterprise at the Spa.

On 17th November, 1735, an agreement for the lease of the lower part of the Walk Field containing the chalybeate spring was drawn up between Sir Edward Southcott and his wife Dame Jane, Dr James Taverner, and Mr Martin Carter for twenty-one years at a yearly rent of £1 to be paid on Christmas Day. The remainder of the field was leased to a Mr Mandeford but in 1741 this ended and Dr Taverner and Mr Carter then rented the whole field from Sir

Edward for another £9 a year.

Sir Edward Southcott and his wife were the owners of Witham Place, a huge mansion in the Powers Hall End area, the only remains of the estate being a brick wall fronting the road and the barn at Spring Lodge.

Taverner describes in his essay of 1738 how the original well produced fresh water and not the chalybeate he knew was near by:

"The spring was first discovered about forty years ago [say, 1695]. But, by digging the well too near the verge of the mineral stratum, and where it was extremely thin; by making the reservoir too large; and by admitting into it, through inadvertence, a spring of common fresh water, the spa soon lost its reputation (for it had been much esteemed, even before it was formed into a regular well) and by degrees grew into disrepute. It had been, for several years, entirely neglected; but, in the year 1736, was again revived; and, by carefully avoiding those mistakes which evidently occasioned the ruin of the former well, it is now fixed to a much better advantage."

The Spa was three quarters of a mile from the town; the spring rose on the side of a gentle slope and close to a fine avenue of lime trees, which extended from Witham Place to the road leading to Falkbourne. The springhead lay twelve feet below the surface. Christy wrote in 1910 that the well no longer existed although he was able to identify the site. The Rev. Canon Ingles, vicar of Witham, assisted him.

"The well was about one hundred yards from, and in front of, the present Spa Place, lying in a meadow on the northern slope of the valley of a tiny

The avenue of lime trees in 1948, now replaced by a housing estate. The spa site was probably where there appears to be a pond in the photograph. The road leading out of the bottom of the picture is Highfields Road.

© Crown Copyright/MOD

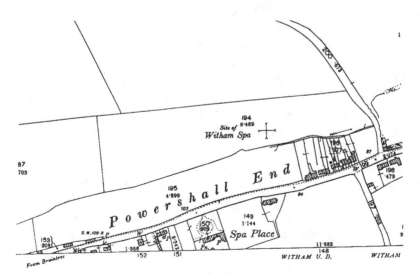

1893 Ordnance Survey Map

rivulet which runs down to the Blackwater River. Its site is, as Taverner says, close to the fine avenue of limes that formerly led down from Witham Place to Faulkbourne. Although the greater part of this avenue has now disappeared, like Witham Place itself, a considerable portion of what was the western end remains, and the site of the well was about a dozen yards to the south-east of the eastern most tree now standing." Here a very slight depression in the turf, about five feet across and scarcely noticeable unless pointed out, was shown to Christy as the site of the well by Mr Quilter, who lived close at hand, and his statement was confirmed by several elderly neighbours, though none could speak positively. "Since then, however Canon Ingles has been informed by a very old woman named Brown, living in Church Street, that she can remember dancing, in her young days, on the wooden trap which then covered the well, and that was the spot in question. She adds that the well has since been closed by a dome of brickwork, over which turf has since been laid.'

What may be the location of the well was found in 1976 during building work on the north-east side of the Spa roundabout. The well was seven feet deep by three feet wide, red bricked and lime mortared and a York stone stepping path led to it. Another sixteen feet deep well was found nearby, which had a stick ditch soak away. These may have been ordinary domestic wells but their position matches Miller Christy's description and there does not seem to be any history of other buildings on the site. We favour this as the site of the Spa. It is private property and the wells are now lost under the houses and garden features.

In his *Essay* dedicated to Dr John Hollings

(1683?-1739), a Physician in Ordinary to His Majesty, stating, "I have endeavoured to give as distinct an Account as I was able of an excellent Mineral Water which, if more known, would be more generally admired", Taverner extolled the virtues of the water thus.

'The Witham Spa is a sulphurous chalybeate water, impregnated with a small quantity of salts, but carrying in it a larger proportion of an alcinate earth; that its virtues, therefore, are not only conformable to those of its several ingredients, but may, likewise, and do, many of them, result from the mixture and united virtues of the whole. As a chalybeate, it quickens the whole circulation, attenuates the blood, dissolves viscid humours, (and) opens obstructions; after which, by its austere and stypick quality, it strengthens the relaxed fibres, recovers the lost tone of the solids and restores their due elasticity. As a sulphurous water, it is, likewise attenuating, resolving, dessicative, balsamick, pectoral, vulnerary, and antiscobutick. From its salts, it incites, stimulates, dissolves, sizy humours, promotes the several sectors, and is, in particular very diuretick.'

He goes on "Thus do these several principles conspire in forming a most useful composition, and from their union results this most excellent mineral water, whose singular virtues and efficacy will render it beneficial in many, if not in most chronic diseases incident to mankind.' Did the good doctor take the waters himself or use his patients for his experiments? He said however that he used his friend `the ingenious Dr Legge, of Braintree' in his experiments.

He assured the readers of his *Essay* that, "In hectick fevers, in constitutions debilitated by long illnesses, in lowness of spirits from a general relaxation of the solids, in weakness of the nerves, in want of appetite and indigestion, in habitual colick and vomiting, in obstructions of several kinds, in agues, in the jaundice and beginning dropsy, in nephritic disorders, in some asthmatick and several scorbutick cases, and many others, too tedious as to mention here, the Witham Spa has been already used with great benefit and success."

That was written not long after the Spa had opened, so it could be wondered just how many people drank the waters and were cured of so many complaints.

He goes on, "But what makes it of less general use is that the mineral spirit is of so exceeding volatile a nature as to make its escape upon carriage, tho' the bottles are ever so carefully corked and cemented; whence it becomes necessary for those who would drink it to advantage to come to the spring and take it upon the spot."

So it was necessary to actually go to Witham to take the water. Here was a man who would have been an asset to most pharmaceutical firms today. His method of advertising was very modern and advanced for his day.

Taverner opened his spa to the public in 1737 and an article in the *Colchester Courier* 23rd June, 1739, said,

'Notice is hereby given that the Witham Spa is now in full perfection and constant attendance will be given at the Well as usual.

"The great and deserved encouragement this excellent mineral water met with last year and the many remarkable cures performed by it of which an account will soon be published, have determined the proprietors to build a Long Room with conveniences for music, dancing etc. that they may contribute as much as in them is as well to the pleasure as to the health of the company. To those who desire to be further acquainted with the nature and vertues of it will find them in Taverner's essay upon the Witham Spa printed about two years ago. Those who design to pass the season are desired to apply in letter to the said Dr Taverner, Mr Martin Carter or Mr Jacob Pattison at Witham in Essex who will provide proper lodgings for them.

"N.B. The situation of the Spa is exceedingly beautiful, the spring arising close to a fine walk of lime trees about a half a mile in length and planted 550 years ago."

The spa was probably advertised in all the newspapers although only advertisements in the *Ipswich Journal* have survived to the present day. The following advertisement appeared on 29 May, 1742.

"Notice is hereby given, that there will be an Assembly at the Long Room at Witham Spa in Essex on Thursday the 24th of the instant June. Tickets to be had at 2s6d each, at the White Hart and Red Lyon at Witham whenever required or at the Little Room next the Pump upon the Day of The Assembly.

"N.B. As the publication of an Account of Cases, wherein the Witham Spa has been successful (which was designed for the press this last Winter) has been postponed for some Reasons not necessary to mention here; it was thought proper, 'til that Design can be executed, to acquaint the Publick in the meantime, that its Efficacy has been fully experienced in the following cases viz. In Hecticks of various Kinds; in Weakness succeeding long

Illnesses; in Lowness of Spirits from a general Relaxing of the Solids; in Weakness of the Nerves; in Want of Appetite; in Indigestion; in habitual Colick and Vomiting; in Obstruction of several kinds; in Agues; in the Jaundice and Beginning Dropsy; in a dangerous Cough and Hectick consequence upon spitting of Blood; in Diabetes; in some Asthmatick, some Nephritic and several Scorbutick Cases; and many other Chronic Disorders, not reducible to any particular Case or Denomination." These words were a repeat of those written earlier but Taverner liked to see his thoughts in print!

There are no physical remains and very little written description of the Spa buildings themselves. However Morant wrote, "the great hall at New Hall (Boreham) was bought and translated here (Witham) for an Assembly Room." John Olmius, who owned The Hall, was demolishing two wings of the building. It is probable that the woodwork, roof tiles, stone and bricks were bought from him and the rooms of the Spa were built from them.

It is from the advertising in the local papers that one can guess that the Spa consisted of a Long Room used for assemblies and balls, a Little Room for tickets and cards and a Pump Room. There were probably cloak-rooms and retiring rooms attached to the main assembly areas. "Spa Place" was built as a residence for a doctor and his patients. This still exists, although in a much altered appearance.

Dr Taverner continued to extol the virtues of his Spa water on 18 June, 1743.

"WITHAM IN ESSEX

The Success of our Spa having equall'd if not exceeded the utmost Hopes that were conceiv'd of it; it is thought proper to acquaint the Publick that constant Attendance is given as usual.

The MONTHLY ASSEMBLIES at the LONG ROOM (the first of which will be on the 23rd of the instant June) are now put upon a Subscription, when by then will be a Certainty of meeting good Company. Any Gentleman or Lady, however, tho' not a Subscriber will find a ready Admittance (the Subscription not being intended to exclude any such) upon signifying their Inclination at the Spa, or at the Red Lyon or White Hart at Witham.

And for the latter Accommodation if any persons who lodge in the Town and have not the convenience of an Equipage, a Hackney Chaise, or Coach, if required will convey them to and from the Spa at an easy Expense.

N.B. The WEEKLY ASSEMBLIES will be continued as formerly.'

The season opened in June and closed in September or October, the dates of the assemblies for the year being advertised in the newspapers in May and then each month during the season. The monthly assemblies or dances were normally held in the Long Room on the first Monday or Thursday of the month but sometimes had to be altered when it clashed with other events. In August, 1743, it was advertised that "our next Monthly Assembly having been fixed the Thursday the 25th; and the horse race at Parslow-Wood-Common, with the Ball at Brentwood being appointed for the same day; it was thought proper, that they might not interfere, to alter our Assembly at the Long Room to Monday the 22nd instant".

Card assemblies were held twice a week whilst a 'Concert of Musick' included in the 2s6d admission sometimes preceded the monthly assemblies. The monthly assemblies were 'kept upon a Subscription with a Design to exclude improper Company' although 'Persons of a Genteel Appearance and Behaviour' would find 'ready Admittance'. Concerts and assemblies were also held in the town but attendance at the events at the spa was encouraged by the provision of transport from local areas 'at an easy expense'. The last assembly of the season was often advertised as being, 'if desired by the subscribers'.

The road from London through Witham was 'as fine a road as any in England' and was served by coaches and carriages from London to Colchester, Ipswich and Harwich although travelling was not always as safe as it is today. In 1743 highwaymen between Lexden and Stanway held up the Colchester coach. Coach travel was becoming more comfortable and by the 1760s the London to Ipswich coach service was advertised as 'coaches hung upon steel springs with no outside passengers whatsoever'.

Dr Taverner died in December, 1746, and the Spa continued with its medicinal functions and social events at least until 1772, but in 1754 the new fashionable craze for sea bathing began to be advertised. The nearest place to Witham was Wivenhoe where baths were owned and promoted by Horace Flacke.

Other sea bathing resorts became established in Essex, one at Harwich and another at Southend-on-Sea where there were other entertainments provided for their customers or patrons.

In 1803 a book, *The Beauties of England and Wales*, said that the chief trade of Witham was from people coming in the summer to drink the spa water, but the former glory of Witham's Spa seemed to have died with its first proprietor, Dr James

Taverner.

Witham was the only town in Essex that became a spa town in the style of Cheltenham or Tunbridge Wells, although it was of course on a much smaller scale. However, the residents used its popularity to 'improve' their houses and many of the Georgian buildings in the town could perhaps ascribe their origins to Dr Taverner and his Spa.

The only reminders of those days now are Spa Place, Spa Road and two houses near the spa site named *Little Spa* and *Taverners* and a display in the Heritage Centre.

Two views of Newland Street, Witham

HOCKLEY SPA

Hockley Spa is the only Essex spa still in evidence. It is a white building standing in Spa Road in Hockley. Construction began in 1842 and it opened to the public in 1843, but was a short-lived attraction, closing a few years later when it became a Baptist chapel. After that it had a chequered history, being turned into a private billiard hall, a clothing factory and various small industrial concerns. It was re-opened by two local brothers who bottled the water, but this too failed. Today it is privately owned and is being renovated, but after such a momentous beginning it was a pity that it did not live up to the hopes and aspirations of its first owners and developers.

Augustus Bozzi Granville (1783-1872) was the first travel writer to describe this spa. Sir Richard Phillips (1767-1840), who had analyzed the water had told him about it. It took Granville a while to locate the Spa but he eventually found a house belonging to Mr Fawcett, solicitor, named *Hockley Spa Lodge*, where he stayed for the night and learned about the discovery of the well that gave Hockley its spa.

Mr and Mrs Clay lived in a cottage near the well and Mr Clay discovered the spring in the garden. They had come from Cheltenham where Mrs Clay took the waters for her asthma. After moving to Hockley she began to drink the spring water and found her health began to improve. Friends took her to another town where her condition became worse and it was not until she returned to Hockley and began to drink the water again that her health returned to normal. Word spread and people began to visit the well for the benefit of their health.

Mr Fawcett publicised the water as a commercial venture. It was sent to London and sold in various chemists' shops and people drank the water to cure their medical conditions. Sir Richard Phillips analyzed the water, which was found to contain common salt, bicarbonate of lime, Epsom salts and sulphate of lime. These chemicals were purported to cure asthma, kidney stones and rickets in children. Sir Richard tasted the liquid himself and proclaimed it to be pleasant and refreshing. He recommended it to everyone and suggested that a hotel should be built and that the well be enclosed in a building provided with baths and a pump room. Mr Fawcett found a number of people in London who were interested in developing the spa and in 1842 the foundation stone for Hockley Spa was laid.

The *Chelmsford Chronicle* printed a report of the laying of the foundation stone on Wednesday, 29th June, 1842. According to the newspaper, the weather that day was fine and the scenery around the site added to the attractions and interest in the proceedings. Mr Fawcett, Mr S Reed, and Mr S Mayne, the three proprietors, along with James Lockyer, the architect, and James Caleb Writtenbury, the builder, gathered for the ceremony.

A procession was led by a band of musicians; the foreman of the works carried the plans; the workmen had the tools of their trade; the builder carried a mallet and square; the architect who had a silver trowel and glass of coins was followed by John Atkinson, Esquire, Deputy of the Ward of Cripplegate Without; Septimus Read, Esquire; Mr S Mayne; and Reverend J Saunders, Curate of Cripplegate. A number of other gentlemen joined them.

These worthies arrived at the stone and the

architect presented Mr Atkinson with a glass bottle containing a set of coins with the head of Queen Victoria on them and vellum with an inscription. This display of pomp and circumstance seems quaint today, but in then it was meant to impress the locals and the reporting of it in the paper was advertising. Mr Atkinson, using the silver trowel, spread the mortar over the aperture containing the bottle and the vellum. After a prayer or two the assemblage of worthies proceeded to a marquee pitched in the field opposite the spa for a cold collation and the day closed to everyone's satisfaction.

The choice of Mr Atkinson to lay the stone seems curious, but Mr Fawcett had aspirations to become an important person in the City of London. He lived in the Ward of Cripplegate Without and Mr Atkinson, who was already Deputy to the Alderman of The Ward of Cripplegate Without may have been useful to an ambitious solicitor.

During the next twelve months the building was completed. Dr Henry Laver, F.S.A., who was living in the vicinity at the time, watched with interest the building of the pump-room which he described as being big enough for Bath. He wrote to Mr Miller Christy that he was very interested in the building and that any half-holiday he got he spent in watching the workmen. He remembered seeing the workmen casting the plaster ornaments for the ceiling. He commented on the fact that it was the first time he had seen Roman Cement used to stucco a wall.

On Thursday, 8th June, 1843, Hockley Spa was opened to the public. This event was accompanied by another ceremony.

The *Chelmsford Chronicle* was represented and, judging by the florid language used in the report of the proceedings, it was written by the same person who described the stone laying ceremony. The reporter even composed a poem extolling the virtues of the spa water.

"Not its unseen depths to dwell
The hermit fountain of some dripping cell.
Its salt of life, which does to all relish give
Its standing pleasure, and intrinsic wealth -
The body's virtue, and their soul's good fortune."

The activities began at two o'clock in the afternoon when one hundred and fifty ladies and gentlemen sat down to breakfast in the pump room. After the toast to the Queen, speeches were made, compliments given and platitudinous votes of thanks were passed between the worthies. Mr Fawcett, the owner, said he had letters of recommendation from Mrs Shaw-Lefevre (later Lady Eversley), wife of the Speaker of the House of Commons, Lady Whitbread and Sir William Stanley. These people had tasted the water and were prepared to speak highly of it. Toasts were drunk to the health and prosperity of the architect, the proprietors, the builders, and Dr Granville, who wrote about the spa in his book *The spas of England.* Dr Granville praised the virtues of the water and wished that the spa would be as successful as everybody hoped. After the speeches ended the room was cleared for dancing. A week later the *Chronicle* published a résumé of the speeches which would make a reader today think that it was more like a mutual admiration society meeting than a ceremony in a small country village laid on to impress the local inhabitants.

The *Chronicle* printed a description of the Spa.

"The pump room is in the Italian style of

architecture. The length of the interior is 43 feet and the breadth nearly 33 feet and it is approached by a noble flight of steps, stretching 20 feet along the front and terminating with chaste pillars, which give to the entrance an aura of great architectural elegance. The interior is beautifully finished, the walls being of a new description of Sienna marble paper by Mr T R Mulcock, (High Street, Newington Butts), the plinth, pilasters and entablature of the niche of Brocatells marble, the cornice of veined marble and the woodwork wainscot of oak. The windows are all of beautiful plate glass, and the splendid marble chimney pieces were executed by Brine. Opposite the landing in a tasteful circular recess, stands the genius of the place - the pump, beautifully formed of satin wood and glass, with a table or counter of veined marble. The centre of the pump is a triumphal arch of satin wood, inlaid with rose wood; the table is one solid block of marble, the handle of yellow glass and the spout silver. It was built by Gallien. Above the back of the pump, in the head of the recess, are represented the constellations, in gold, under which the first stone was laid and the building commenced; it has a very excellent effect and was designed by Mr Lockyer. The whole appearance of the building, with its two cloakrooms and other requisite apartments, bespeaks the highest credit upon the skill and judgement of Mr Lockyer, the architect."

The whole report is included because it appears that little expense was spared to furnish the pump room. It reeks of Victorian keeping up with the Joneses or at least with other well known spas in England or Europe. If you could see the pump room in its present ruinous state you would wonder what

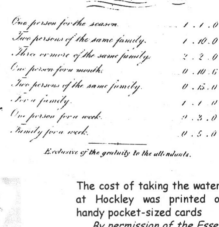

One person for the season.	1 . 1 . 0
Two persons of the same family.	1 . 10 . 0
Three or more of the same family.	2 . 2 . 0
One person for a month.	0 . 10 . 6
Two persons of the same family.	0 . 15 . 0
For a family.	1 . 1 . 0
One person for a week.	0 . 3 . 0
Family for a week.	0 . 5 . 0

Exclusive of the gratuity to the attendants.

The cost of taking the waters at Hockley was printed on handy pocket-sized cards
By permission of the Essex Record Office

Bottles of Hockley Water could be bought in the 1980s

happened to those fittings.

The proprietor, Mr Fawcett, had an apparatus erected to give the water an aerated form so as to render it pleasanter than soda water and from its aperient qualities much more beneficial when taken instead of the soda water. In the publicity that was sent to outlets in London and other parts of England claims were made that the water was beneficial in complaints of the digestive organs, afflictions of the liver and kidneys and rickets in children. There were druggists' shops in Essex and London, including Sheens in Vauxhall, Whites in Cornhill and Jacksons in Cheapside to name just a few chemists who had supplies of the Hockley water to sell to their customers. The *Essex Chronicle* published a list of more than fifty outlets from where the liquid could be purchased.

You could take the water at the spa at prices varying from 3 shillings for one person per week to 2 guineas for a family for the season.

Following the opening of the spa to the public a hotel was built at the junction of the Rayleigh, Rochford and Southend roads. The hotel was and still is a two-storey building with stables and coach houses behind it. Other villas and lodging houses were erected near the spa.

Despite the hopes and aspirations of the proprietors and the publicity printed in the *Chelmsford Chronicle* the spa, the hotel and villas declined in use very quickly.

A woman of a strong healthy appearance was employed to dispense the water to the customers in the hope that her robust figure would convince them that the water had a good effect on the body. However, the result of all this enterprise was most

Hockley Spa before the adjoining house was built

The Spa Hotel was built to accommodate the expected hoards of visitors

discouraging to the proprietors. The public withheld its patronage and refused to come and be cured. There were a few visitors, but there was nothing for them to see or do, and they just wandered about and looked miserable. At this time railways were being opened all over the country, which made access easier to the more fashionable watering places of Matlock, Buxton, Bath, and even spas on the continent. Hockley Spa declined well before the opening of the railway line from Brentwood to Southend, which did not reach Hockley until 1st October, 1889.

The announcement of the sale of the Spa Hotel appeared in the *Chelmsford Chronicle* of 19th May, 1848. Posters were displayed in public houses in Essex and London and in Fawcett's, the proprietor's practice. The pump room was also put up for sale but it was delayed and it was reported that the undertaking proved wholly unremunerative and quickly collapsed. Benton, writing in 1871, stated that the whole place had then a most dilapidated appearance; the hotel had been let at £10 per annum as a beer shop; and the unfortunate spa room was used as a Baptist chapel.

In about 1880 Mr Laveaux, a French gentleman living in London, contemplated re-establishing the spa and he spent some time and £20 cleaning out the well and obtaining an analysis of the water; but his efforts came to nothing.

About twelve years later, another effort was made to develop the spa by means of a Limited Liability Company, a prospectus of which was issued. Mr Coghlan, and Mr Beck, both of London, were among the directors. Once more, the scheme failed.

In 1904 the spa passed into the ownership of Mr J H Burgess who used it as part of his house, which adjoined the pump room. It was redecorated and converted into a billiard room for his private use but visitors to Hockley were still able to drink the water free of charge. Mr Burgess had the water analyzed and its quality was said to be as good as ever it was.

After Burgess's death, the contents of the property were sold by auction in 1944. In 1945 Schweppes, who currently market Malvern Water, bought the spa. Nothing came from their ownership and they sold the property in 1950.

Since 1950 the spa has had many uses. It became a printing works and a clothes factory. In 1967 demolition was considered, but in 1972 the spa was listed as a Grade 2 building.

The next important date in the history of the spa was in 1980 when Guinness Bros. (Snooker Specialists) Ltd. bought it. The owners repaired and repainted the building and while they were repairing the floor they rediscovered the well. In 1981 they decided to launch a company to sell the mineral water. The well could produce 2,000 gallons of water per week. In 1984 the brothers began to bottle the water and made their first deliveries in May that year. The company was named Hockley Spa Mineral Water Company Ltd. An advertisement worded in Victorian style stated that, "The proprietors of the Hockley Spa Mineral Water Company deem it their duty in bringing this pure Spa Water before the public generally to state from the high testimonials given by medical men of its medicinal qualities, that they are desirous of extending its benefits by delivery direct to residents in the South East from Monday, May 21, 1984. For only 40p. per litre bottle. This beautifully clear water contains elements for a natural healthy life, *e.g.* calcium, magnesium, zinc, potassium, sulphate, iron, etc."

Despite an initial interest from a local super-market and the reported signing of contracts with a Japanese company this business was not a success. The company went into liquidation and by 1989 the spa had changed hands several times. Local councillors viewed the site in April to see whether it was feasible to change the spa and its associated building into a nursing home. When it was put on the market for sale, planning permission was given for that purpose - but no one bought it. When the writers of this book visited the spa it was in a very ruinous state.

There were pigeons flying about the pump room, the walls were badly stained by water coming through the roof and the floor was covered in grime and bird droppings. What a come down! It was very difficult to imagine the pump room as it had been in 1843.

In the 1990s it was sold by auction and its present owners are trying hard to renovate and restore the building to its former glory. The outside of the spa building has been painted, the house has been refurbished and work is now proceeding on the roof and the inside of the spa building. This is all proving to be rather costly and the owners are looking for grants to help pay for the restoration. We understand that Hockley water may be available again in the not-too-distant future. All the buildings of Hockley Spa can still be seen from Spa Road, near Hockley Station.

THE CHALYBEATE SPRING AT DOVERCOURT SPA

The water feeding the well in the spa at Dovercourt began as a small stream of fresh water issuing from the cliff and running down to the sea. The Romans may have used it, as finds from that period were on display in the museum in the spa building. In 1670 the stream was noticed and tasted by the antiquary, Silas Taylor, who said that it was a spring of excellent, clear, and delightful water, coming from the side of the cliff and it was approved by those men who had the ability to judge such qualities.

Two hundred years later John Bagshaw, who was Member of Parliament for Harwich in 1847, saw Dovercourt, then a small village of about fifty cottages, as an ideal setting for a spa town similar to Scarborough, which had (and still has) its own spa. In 1845 he built a large house called Cliff House and it was in the grounds of that house he rediscovered the chalybeate spring. He ordered his architect W H Lindsey to plan an extensive and impressive cliff top development including a spa building, pump room, museum, reading room and library. Lindsey was not the only architect involved in this development. A local architect named Horace Darken had submitted plans for a building that would be built below the cliff so that the view from Orwell Terrace was not obstructed. The firm of James Butterworth of Ipswich also published plans of plots of land for housing around the spa.

However, the development that became a reality was Orwell Terrace, two hotels and the spa complex, which opened to the public on 28th August, 1854, the day the Eastern Counties Railway Company celebrated the opening of its railway to Harwich. Following this

Dovercourt Spa

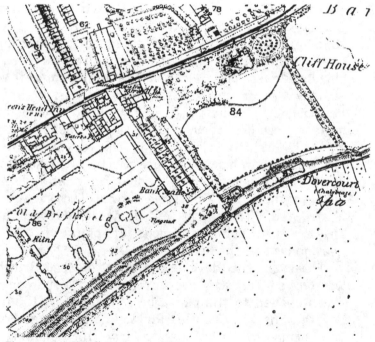

The Spa and Orwell Terrace in 1893

ceremony some of the dignitaries boarded the steamers *Prince* and *River Queen* and viewed the spa from the sea whilst others went to the spa itself. All admired the building and several glasses of the water were drunk which was found to be refreshing on such a warm and sultry day if not particularly medically beneficial.

Taylor had mentioned the medical properties of the water in 1670 as being endorsed by people who knew about them. When John Bagshaw opened the spa, Mr M Lever, a chemist from London, analyzed the water and found that it contained oxide of iron, carbonate and sulphate of lime, carbonate and sulphate of magnesium and chloride of sodium that was similar to the water of Tunbridge Wells, except for the large quantity of iron that came from the pyrites in the cliffs.

It was written that "The spa water when fresh drawn is bright and sparkling, it is by no means unpleasant to the palate; producing no sort of constitutional disturbance..."

It seemed to have immediate effects on the system producing similar relief that a tonic or digestive remedy would have had. In a guide published in the 1850's it was written that the water should be taken warm, whether it was the water or the patient that should be warm was not stated. The effects of the chalybeate on the system were said to be perspiration, increased secretion of every sort, stimulation and invigoration. It was also suggested that the water was best drunk first thing in the morning whilst taking gentle exercise, followed by a light breakfast. The patient should begin with two or three glasses in the course of the day, gradually increasing the dose until the effects mentioned became apparent. Patients were also advised to use the boating facilities or to take walks in the beautiful gardens.

Charges for using the spa facilities, reading room, saloon and walks went from as much as 1/6d per day for a large family down to sixpence for a single person. Annual and other period tickets could be bought and the toll for entrance to the walks was a penny per person. The price per glass in 1877 was a halfpenny. The reading room provided books from Mudie's Library and a selection of newspapers and periodicals was available to subscribers.

The upkeep of the facilities was maintained by subscribers and by visitors to the hotels in Dovercourt and Harwich. Mrs Jarrold was in charge in the early days, but then for more than twenty years until the early 1890s, the secretary was James Richard Franks with Mrs Mary Elizabeth Jarrold as superintendent. The first proprietor was Henry Warren, who in 1895 was responsible for the maintenance of the interior of the pump room, reading room and furnishings therein. In 1904 the official corporation guide mentioned that there was a small museum containing a collection of Roman remains and fossils discovered in the neighbourhood.

The Spa house was described as -

"A pretty building, erected on a broad walled terrace at the base of the cliff, sheltered from all northerly winds and immediately above the high water mark of the beautiful bay which flows from the German Ocean. It is an ornamental cottage, something in the style of a Pompeian Villa. Its wings form two bays, between which the projecting roof, supported by pillars, covers a verandah furnished with seats for the wearied. The interior consists of

DOVERCOURT SPA

Subscriptions to the
SPA, READING ROOM, SALOON & WALKS

Tickets not transferable may be had at the Spa or of any of the Committee.

FOR A FAMILY ¶ Exceeding Four Persons.				A FAMILY Not exceeding 4 Persons.				ONE PERSON			
	£	s.	d.		£	s.	d.		£	s.	d.
*Annual	2	2	0	Annual	1	10	0	Annual	1	1	0
Six Months	1	10	0	Six Months	1	1	0	Six Months	1	15	0
One Month	0	15	0	One Month	0	12	0	One Month	0	5	0
A Week	0	6	0	A Week	0	5	0	A Week	0	2	0
A Day	0	1	6	A Day	0	1	0	A Day	0	0	6

The Toll for entrance to the Walks 1d. each Person

THE READING ROOM

is supplied with the *Times, Daily News, Standard, Punch, Guardian Illustrated London News, Graphic, Queen, Field, Saturday Review, East Anglian Newsman, Essex Standard,* and a variety of Books from MUDIE'S Library with other Volumes. The Books must on no account be taken from the premises. ¶ A Family includes relations who dwell habitually in the house, and children in charge of attendants.

* Annual Subscribers by the additional payment of 10/6 may introduce, free of charge, *bona fide* Visitors who may be staying in their house.
Annual Tickets date from any quarter, and for Officers of the Army and Navy, quarterly Tickets are issued.
The Rooms are closed on Sundays, but the Walks are available.
The Flowers and Fruits must not be touched;
Smoking is allowed in the Conservatory, but not in the Rooms.
Children must be in charge of a responsible attendant, and be paid for.
The Committee reserve the right of closing the Rooms to Subscribers on special occasions.
The Rooms may be hired on moderate terms by arrangement with the Secretary.

Hon. Sec. J. R. FRANKS

Spa facilities advertised in a local almanac of 1885

By permission of Essex Record Office

43

three principal rooms; the central apartment is of considerable length; well adapted for exercise in warm, cold or wet weather, being ventilated with ample windows commanding beautiful sea views. In the Pump Room, for the purpose of drawing water from the cliff, is a dolphin-head bracket, on which, in a niche in the wall, stands a vase filled with choice flowers; underneath where the water is drawn, a shell basin receives the surplus. The other wing of the building forms a similar room, intended for a library, from which a handsome stained glass door, containing a beautiful portrait of Queen Elizabeth - the great patroness of Harwich - opens into a conservatory filled with choice plants in blossom, and further on is a small Italian garden; from this garden, passing under a rather quaint archway, a series of steps lead up to the New Town of Dovercourt, which is within a minute's walk of the Spa."

The enthusiasm shown by Bagshaw for the development of Dovercourt as a spa town and bathing resort could not be maintained and in 1859, when he was near bankruptcy, the site was sold to the Woods and Forest Department and the building of the new town ceased.

The spa continued to be owned and used by the Woods and Forests Department until 1910 when it was leased to the Council for 31 years from 5th January, at an annual rent of £100. The spa was mainly disused, but plans were drawn up to refurbish it. In April, 1910, £675 was to be given towards the repairs to the roof and for public conveniences to be built. Although plans were accepted from Messrs. Cheal and Sons of Crawley, Surrey, and Mr Stewart Watling, of Dovercourt they were deferred until the autumn of that year.

The bandstand on Dovercourt promenade erected in 1902

Choice plants filled the conservatory attached to the Spa

Whilst these plans were being discussed it was proposed by the council that Mr Warren, previously described as the proprietor, would not carry on with his duties and the post was advertised, the position being described as caretaker. The conditions relating to the duties of caretaker were issued and this is what they were;

(1) The corporation will pay all Rates and taxes: keep The Gardens in order; provide all Furniture for the Pump Room and Reading Room, and Daily and Weekly Papers and Periodicals for the latter room.

(2) The Manager shall supply a trustworthy 'Toll Taker' (or more than one on Bank Holidays and other occasions, if necessary) and shall charge each person passing through the grounds or entering the Pump Room the sum of 1d. per diem. He shall also charge to each person using the Reading Room the sum of 2d. per diem (or 1/- per week to include admission and Reading Room.)

(3) He shall give a ticket to each person and shall account to the Borough Surveyor on each Monday for all Tolls and Entrance fees received by him.

(4) He shall keep the Pump Room and Reading Room and the furniture therein properly cleaned and dusted and shall be responsible for the proper management thereof. He shall lay out the papers each morning and remove the ones out of date. He shall also keep the Grounds of the Spa clean and free from litter.

(5) He shall lock up the Spa premises each night at 10 o'clock or at such other times as may be fixed by The Pleasure Grounds Committee and, as far as possible, shall prevent any damage to Corporate

property, or to the Automatic Machines placed in the Grounds.

(6) He shall have the privilege of providing Teas or other refreshments (except intoxicating Liquors) and to use, for this purpose, the Pump Room and terraces to the Eastward thereof.

(7) A ladies' Lavatory will be provided and shall be kept clean and in good order by the Manager, a penny in the slot lock, the takings from which shall go to the Corporation, therein shall secure the 'Convenience'. The manager shall be entitled to charge 3d. for a Wash and Brush up; but must supply clean Towels, Soap and Hot Water etc. at his own cost and trouble.

It seemed that Mr Warren would be hiring the Spa for several years at £20 per annum subject to certain repairs and alterations being made.

In June, 1910, Mr Watling prepared plans for alterations to the existing spa buildings and an alternative plan for rebuilding the premises was considered. Tenders were invited for the work, but in 1911 it was proposed to demolish the Spa.

The buildings were considered to be unsightly and dangerous and it was thought that a new edifice could be constructed for concert parties and band performances whose organisers would lease them. In May, 1911, the Council wanted to borrow £2,000 to restore the spa and gardens, but once again the plans were postponed. The Spa and Gardens were cleared and made as attractive as possible for the summer season, and the tolls were increased and the gardens known as Cliff Park were re-opened on George V's Coronation Day (22nd June). Later in the year Mr Saunders was paid £41.15.9d for repairs and Mr Brown accepted the duties of caretaker.

This is how the money was spent on the refurbishment of the Spa and gardens.

Painting and repairs to the spa	£8. 6. 3
Repairs to park and lavatories	£43.11. 5
Repairs to lavatories	£3. 9. 4
Repairs to spa well	£2. 5. 6
Payment to Cheal and Son	£117.17. 4
Payment to Cobb (repairs)	£7.10. 5
Willson - newspapers for reading room	£2. 4. 2
Parsons & Co - Furniture	£6.15. 0
Pontifex & Co - Lamp columns for park	£26.19. 6
Total	£218.18.11

More repairs and renovations were carried out and twelve beach huts were built at the western end of the gardens to bring in more revenue.

So the Spa continued until the outbreak of war in 1914 when a unit of the Essex Fortress Royal Engineers (T) (Electricals) took over the coastal defences and half the company was billeted in the spa building until 1919. In April, 1919, the Quartering Committee asked the Council to submit a claim for damages. The Borough Surveyor prepared an estimate of £464.14.5d and £419.19.0 was eventually agreed.

In August, 1919, a committee was convened to consider re-opening the museum and replacing the assembly buildings. In September the Borough Surveyor declared that the buildings were no longer safe and the Council agreed that they should be demolished. A prize of £52.10.0 was offered for plans for the new construction, but none was forthcoming so the whole Dovercourt Spa was demolished in 1920 without replacement.

All that marks the former site is a plaque on the esplanade where a few tiles from the Spa building were set in the pavement, but even these have disappeared, probably thrown into a skip by workmen during repairs to the path.

Of the three spas built in Essex that at Dovercourt lasted the longest, due perhaps to its opening coinciding with the arrival of the railway and the development of the town as a seaside resort for all classes of people who took their annual holidays there, the spa being one of the attractions.

Dovercourt Spa

THE MINERAL WATERS OF VANGE

'The Vale of Health: The Magic Wells discovered by Edwin Cash in 1898' was painted on a large signboard near the *Five Bells* public house on the London Road in Vange. It was used to advertise one of two mineral waters available for sale to the public in the 1920s.

It was the brainchild of a publican, Edwin Cash, who ran the *Angel Hotel*, Islington, although the history of the well began in 1898 when Mr King of Hovells Farm found a damp place in a field and dug a well. He tried the water, but didn't like the taste. However, a dry summer persuaded him to give the water to his cattle which thrived on it. News of this water and its beneficial qualities reached Mr Cash. He arranged to have the water analyzed in 1901. The analyst, Dr Rideal, found high concentrations of sulphates of magnesium, sodium and potassium. He suggested that this showed that the water was of medicinal quality and could be suitable for children suffering from rickets, and nearly all stomach complaints; Cash offered to buy the farm but had to make do with part of the estate.

In 1919 Cash retired from the *Angel* and decided to develop the well. A second well was dug and a large wooden hut was erected. A limited company, The Vange Water Company, was set up in 1921 with registered offices in 2, Foster Lane, Cheapside, London, EC2. The bottled water sold for two shillings and threepence at local chemists in Essex.

The pint sized bottles were short and made of clear glass with a label on the front bearing the words 'Vange Water' in large letters and 'The Vale of Health' in smaller letters. The label on the other side gave a lengthy description of the qualities and purity of the contents. It was described as 'A natural product of England' and it was claimed to be a cure for any digestive ailment. The dosage recommended was one wineglassful, but an overdose could only have beneficial results. The bottle itself was embossed with the name 'Vange Water'.

Then in 1922 the national newspapers heard about the Vange water. Under the headline of WONDER WELL IN AN ESSEX VILLAGE the *Westminster Gazette* reported that a George Murrell, aged over 80 years, who used the water for making his tea, had found the well (which made two claimants for the discovery). After drinking it he felt better than he had ever been for more than twenty years. The story was linked with another about Mr Monson, a London radiographer and X-ray specialist, who was claiming that Southend mud had remarkable medicinal properties. It was hoped to build hydros at Southend and Vange and get Southend Council funding to build a spa at Vange. After this publicity hoards of people flocked to Vange to drink the water. Queues formed to taste and buy bottles of the liquid to take home.

Mr Cash, or Farmer Cash as he became known, put up a large sheet for people to throw their money in as payment for the glass of water. Orders came from all over Britain and the two wells were hard put to maintain the supply. So a limit of 10 gallons per day only was reserved for callers to purchase and 90 gallons were used for bottling and orders sent in. It was this portioning of the supply that led to a notice being put up one day stating that the water for the day had been sold and someone reporting to the *Westminster Gazette* that the wells in Vange had dried up. This was published in the paper on October 10th, 1922, and proved disastrous to Edwin Cash and his company. Mr Cash began libel proceedings against the paper, but the case was settled out of court and the Vange Water Company accepted payment of costs by the newspaper.

The libel case was not concluded until May, 1923, but business had not come to an end in October, 1922. The water continued to be advertised in the local newspapers.

The shed was said to be packed with green bottles waiting to be filled. It has been suggested that a change to green bottles was made because the water had turned cloudy. A third well was dug. When this collapsed a fourth well was dug and, when this did not give the expected yield, a fifth was excavated. This fifth well was obviously considered to be the final one as a building in the style of a Greek temple was built to enclose it. The temple was inscribed with the names 'Vange Well 5' and 'Vange Water Company'. Mr Cash took advantage of the General Election by sending three bottles of the water to Andrew Bonar Law with the advice that, if he took the water, he would win the election. Bonar Law won the election, but we don't know how much Vange water contributed to his success.

Local people still remember the well and recall stories of its wonders. One couple remembered that, "We went for a picnic and my grandmother, she had a bottle of this Vange water and after she drank it she started dancing and she said that it was the Vange waters that had done it because it had supposed to been so good."

The *Grays and Tilbury Gazette* topped this with its own story. "One is constantly hearing of the marvellous cures wrought by the newly discovered Vange water. The latest story told to me is that of an aged lady who had been bedridden for five years. Recently she tried a bottle of the precious liquid and was able to get up and go to a whist drive a few nights ago. Some day, perhaps, a special strong variety will be found which will raise the dead.'

Meanwhile, a rival had appeared on the scene. The Vange Crystal Well Company was set up at Luncies Farm by another Mr King. The water was extracted from a well he used previously as a domestic supply. The report of the analysis of the water by one of the leading analysts in London stated that it was a highly medicinal water and equal to the great continental waters. The company claimed to have sales of many hundreds of bottles a week. There may have been other rivals and there were suggestions that water from Hockley was sold as Vange water.

Edwin Cash's reaction was to publish an advertisement, which appeared in the *Grays and Tilbury Gazette* on 11th November, 1922.

A WARNING TO GRAYS
AND TILBURY
IMPORTANT STATEMENT BY MR. EDWIN
CASH OF VANGE
It has come to my notice that water pur-
porting to come from my well is being
sold in Grays and Tilbury under the name of
Vange Water. THIS IS TO NOTIFY THE
PUBLIC THAT ONLY WATER WHICH
COMES FROM THE MIRACLE WELL AT
VANGE, which has been analysed for the
past twenty years, and created a recent sensa-
tion in the Press, CAN BE OBTAINED FROM
JORDAN BROTHERS, 50 HIGH STREET, AND
2, NEW ROAD, GRAYS. TAKE CARE THAT

MR. CASH'S SIGNATURE AND PHOTO-
GRAPH ARE ON EACH BOTTLE, OTHER-
WISE YOU WILL BE RECEIVING IMITA-
TIONS.
(SIGNED) EDWIN CASH
Brook House Farm
Fobbing
Essex

An answer to this diatribe appeared in the same
paper the following week.
NOTICE!
GENUINE VANGE WATER
FROM THE WONDER WELL AT VANGE
We desire the public to know that the
Medicated Water offered by us under a
BLUE LABEL is the only genuine VANGE
WATER on the market.
Our water is drawn from a well at
LUNCIES FARM, VANGE that is the
ONLY MEDICATED WELL in Vange. There-
fore, all other offers cannot be from water
taken from Vange, notwithstanding ALL
STATEMENTS to the contrary.
Be careful that you get a bottle with a
BLUE LABEL THEREON, obtainable at -
GRAYS PHARMACY,
J.C. MITCHELL,
58, HIGH STREET, GRAYS.
VANGE CRYSTAL WELL COMPANY
Luncies Farm, Vange near Pitsea.

Mr Mitchell's chemist shop was the oldest in
Grays, having been established for 40 years. Mr
Mitchell himself, described as being of a retiring

Vange Well No. 5 was still in good shape in the early 1950s

disposition, had died in October so perhaps this was a more aggressive form of marketing by the new management.

To understand the argument you need to know that Farmer Cash's well, although being on the Vange Hall Estate, was actually in the parish of Fobbing and not in Vange at all.

But then disaster struck at Luncies Farm. The Sanitary Inspector reported to Billericay Rural District Council in January, 1923, that the water was unfit for domestic consumption owing to its high mineral content. He did not comment on what medical value this might have. It was also said that there was some organic material in the water. Mr H W Rymer of the Vange Crystal Well Company argued that the water was not bottled direct from the well, but was thoroughly treated first. However, it seemed that the public had got the impression that the water offered for sale in the bottles was unsafe to drink and trade was adversely affected and so the company went out of business. The well was closed in March.

Mr Cash's advertisements continued to appear throughout 1923, but perhaps the business was tainted by the problems at Luncies Farm and no more was heard of Vange water after 1924. The property was put up for sale in 1926. Lot 23 was described as being several parcels of land on the Vange estate, particularly in the north-west corner in which were the celebrated medicinal springs with pump room and appurtenances comprising two force pumps as fixed, five inside fixed tanks, also three rainwater tanks outside.

The site of the hoarding has disappeared under the widened A13, but the Vange Water Company's

Remains of the Vange wells in 1993

buildings remained intact until the 1960s. The bottling shed has now gone although the foundations can still be seen. The temple is still there but the domed roof and pillared sides are sadly falling down and the building has seriously deteriorated in the past five years. The site can be reached by following the path across the road opposite the information centre at One Tree Hill, down to the bottom of the valley where you can see the remains on the right. A group is being formed to try to save the building with the assistance of Thurrock Museum, but it is likely that they are now past saving. An attempt to get the remaining building listed by English heritage was unsuccessful.

Luncies Farm was demolished in 1955 as part of the development of Basildon New Town and a church has since been built on the site.

The Vange wells were announced by the sign standing by the main road near the Five Bells

SPRING CLEAR - WICKHAM BISHOPS

Can you imagine yourself as an Iron Age man looking for water in the Wickham Bishops area and finding a clear spring bubbling from the ground? This spring may have made you decide where to build your settlement.

A long time later the Romans used the spring as a watering place on their way from Colchester to the salt pans at Maldon and today it is used, not for the local water supply, but as the source of 'Spring Clear' spring water drinks.

Wickham Bishops spring rises from the ground by the 15th tee on the Benton Hall golf course and feeds into the River Blackwater. The spring supplied water to the Wickham Bishops railway station (that closed on 7th September, 1964) and to cottages in the area and, more recently, has been used for irrigation of the owner's apple orchard.

The 'Spring Clear' drinks are produced by Spring Cool Soft Drinks. Simon Beale and Geoff Chapman started the company as a water purification business in Hadleigh, but, when the owner of both the orchard and the spring brought the supply to their attention, they moved to Wickham Bishops.

The two men took over construction of the plant from small beginnings. From an old apple store and a shed they now possess a plant that can process up to 250 bottles a minute but usually fills and labels 175 bottles in the same time.

The water is piped 600 yards up through the orchard to the company's premises off Langford Road. It is now the only licensed commercial flowing spring in East Anglia and has to comply with all the health regulations that hadn't even been thought of when earlier waters were bottled. Sample water is sent for analysis on a weekly basis and is examined by government scientists three times a year.

Supplies of water are still being used to irrigate the orchards and it is different from other spring waters in this book, as no claims have ever been made that it is a mineral water with any medicinal use.

The first water that was bottled was supplied as 'Spring Clear' fruit flavoured, sparkling drinks sold to schools in 1991 but in 1997 the pure spring water was marketed in a blue bottle with an elegant label. However, the plain Wickham Bishops water was not successful and has been withdrawn from the market. The fruit flavoured drinks have proved to be so successful that they are now also sold in bottles with "sports caps" that young people think are "really cool". These have to be sold as still drinks as sparkling drinks would blow the cap. The drink is also modem in its presentation because it is vitamin enriched and low calorie.

This is a thriving small industry producing a product that is now found in shops, schools and canteens all over Britain and it is exported to several overseas countries, including some in the Middle East. In the modern competitive market new products are needed all the time and Simon and Geoff have now come up with an even more innovative bottle design, a bottle which contains a bendy straw as an integral part of the product that can be removed after the water has been drunk and used as a construction toy. This will surely prove a best seller.

It is interesting to think that the bottling plant at Wickham Bishops produces a drink of spring water flavoured with fruit juices and with no added sugar, a modern concept, of a healthy drink. In fact, it could be considered to be the modern equivalent of the mineral water bottled at Tilbury more than two hundred years ago. Like Tilbury water it is sold in the export market. Essex spring waters have come back to where they started.

Wickham Bishops Water was marketed in blue bottles in 1997

VANISHED WELLS

Besides the principal mineral water supplies in Essex, namely those of Witham, Dovercourt and Hockley Spas and the bottled water of West Tilbury, Vange and Spring Cool there were many lesser springs that during the seventeenth and eighteenth centuries were purported to have curative properties. None of these exists today. Urban sprawl and advances in medical treatment rendered them redundant. Technical advances in local water supplies led to the disuse of wells and springs in gardens and fields. St. Chad's Well and Havering Well have plaques marking the site, but for the remainder the "X" marking the spot has to be guessed at from references in books or names on old maps.

The London area had many springs, some medicinal, some just for supplying homes. Today, those that purported to have medicinal properties have vanished under housing and industrial developments.

HAVERING WELL

In 1783 Martin Trinder mentioned the springs at what is now Roneo Corner. He suggested that amongst other things, the water would retard the onset of gout.

Miller Christy visited the site in 1907 and found that the water ran into a ditch on the east side of the road from Romford to Rainham Ferry. The water collected in a small barrel that was let into the ground so that the top was level with the surface. The land behind the Roneo factory, formerly the Ormond Cycle Works, was full of springs that gave the Roneo firm a lot of trouble with flooding over several years but Christy was unable to identify the exact position of the springhead for the Havering Well. He was told that the water was still reputed to have medicinal value, especially as a cure for sore eyes. However, analysis of a sample he took showed the water to be perfectly ordinary.

The spring has now gone, as has the Roneo factory, but it is commemorated in a small garden just around the corner, named Havering Well Garden.

WOODFORD WELLS

Woodford Wells is the only nameplace in Essex to preserve the memory of the fame of its local wells, which were popular in the early eighteenth century.

The first mention of the wells appeared in the book by Dr Benjamin Allen in 1711 where he describes some experiments done on water samples. In 1722 Samuel Goldsmith, innkeeper of Woodford Row, was granted a licence to erect a coach house and stable adjoining the end of his house known as 'The Sign of the Wells'. This is the earliest reference to an inn in the vicinity, but the actual site of the wells is unknown.

A survey map of Woodford Wood, made in 1757, showed wells named as New Wells and Old Wells situated on the west side of the main road from London to Epping. In 1796 Daniel Lysons wrote that the well was near the nine-mile stone in the forest. The milestone was about 100 yards south of the Horse and Groom inn. This description does not rule out the Old and New Wells, but the Ordnance Survey placed the site north of the Horse and Groom (now the Horse and Well) and to the east of the main road. This site was a hollow place in a meadow where clay was dug for brick making. The green has now been built on. Miller Christy, however, in 1907 visited one other well which was near the nine-mile stone. This well was about 200 yards east of the main road and fitted with a pump and was bricked round with small bricks which he thought looked old. He took a sample for analysis and concluded that it would have had no medicinal value. This has also been built over.

So there were several possible sites for the famous wells.   The water at Woodford Wells had been known as a purging well and as a cure for many ills despite Christy's analysis. It had a reputation as a place for day trips from London for rest and recuperation and other leisure activities and was near to Epping Forest where hunting was popular. But the attractions at Woodford Wells had ended by the end of the eighteenth century.

It seems likely that there was more than one well at Woodford; there are still plenty of ponds in the area. Perhaps Miller Christy didn't sample the right one. Wherever they were they have all disappeared now and it is likely that, despite their reputation, they were never commercially developed.

CHIGWELL ROW

Perhaps this was a spa that never came to be. Someone had great plans that never came to fruition.

In the early part of the eighteenth century there was a well on the hillside behind the windmill to the south of the main road. The water had a purging quality and was highly recommended by a Dr Frewin.

Christy said that the well and windmill no longer existed when he wrote in 1910 but was told by the legendary oldest inhabitant that the well had been in a meadow called Park Field not far from Grange Hill Station. A Mr College could remember it as being in a hollow place, bricked round, with steps leading down to the water. It was known locally as 'The Purging Well'.

Christy later acquired a manuscript that appeared to be a draft of a pamphlet publicising the Chigwell Row Springs rather like those advertising the contemporaneous wells at Witham and Tilbury. He believed the author to have been Dr Martin Trinder and that it was written around 1775.

The manuscript claimed an ancient provenance for the wells by explaining that the name Chigwell derived from the Saxon form of King's Well. It goes on to describe three wells, two near the windmill, one of these apparently that remembered by Mr College, and the third behind a house called White Hall, near the Maypole Inn. The manuscript continued with lengthy details of chemical tests and accounts of wonderful cures that these waters effected.

Dr Trinder apparently had hopes of promoting a new spa, but it seems that the pamphlet was never published. Nothing came of this publicity and all traces of these wells have disappeared. The site of the original well is marked on the large scale Ordnance Survey map as King's Well at the back of Brocket Way. The ground has still not been built on. The site of the third well is commemorated in the name Whitehall Close.

UPMINSTER WELL

Another well that has disappeared is that known as the Upminster Well. Christy wrote that the well at the northern end of Tyler's Common had been famed as a medicinal one for a long period. It was mentioned in Dr Benjamin Allen's book in 1699 and in Trinder's in 1783. In 1907 it was still well preserved and protected by a triangular wooden fence. The sample of water taken by Christy was found to have a high concentration of magnesium and he therefore considered it to be a genuine mineral spring. All that remains now is a depression in a piece of boggy ground.

St Chad's Well

In Billet Road, near Ilford, is a plaque erected in 1951, commemorating the spring that was dedicated to St Chad and which may well have given its name to Chadwell Heath.

It was said to have been a reputable medicinal well and was at one time resorted to by people with weak eye-sight, for special properties of the water were supposed to have been beneficial to the eyes.

The well lay quite solitary on the roadside, partly protected by an alcove of brickwork. Its appearance was so strange at dusk that people said that horses shied away from it.

The water was claimed to be of excellent quality; it had never failed, and there was a constant running off of the surplus. It was once the only water supply to the few cottages nearby. The well went by the name of Brick Well, the Bricken Well (Old English plural form), or the Wooden Well, according to local usage.

Mr Christy visited the well and observed that there was a dome of brickwork that looked as though it was made in the eighteenth century and in good repair. The dome stood by the roadside ditch but the spring was said to be in the field, about 50 yards away. He said the water was clear and neither smelled nor had any taste, There is, however, no sign of the wellhead today. The site of the well is on private property nearby and nothing remains except a depression in some marshy reed covered ground.

WANSTEAD SPA

This was first mentioned in 1619 when John Chamberlain (1553-1627) wrote to Sir Dudley Carleton (later Viscount Dorchester) relating how a new spring had become popular at Wanstead, but that the source was drying up through over-use. Apparently the water compared favourably with that at Tunbridge Wells.

The site of the spa is completely unknown. Miller Christy's friend spoke to the oldest inhabitant of Wanstead, a Mr Morgan, in the late nineteenth century who told him that the only well he had heard of was in Blake Hall Road. The water was chalybeate and left a reddish stain on the earth.

However, Winifred Phillips has put forward the very plausible theory that the spa was in the grounds of Wanstead House, perhaps in the vicinity of the grotto. If it had been in the private grounds of the house only the lords and ladies and other great people would have had the opportunity to visit it. If the well had been in a more public place one might have expected some tradition or folk memory of its site to remain but nothing remains of the spa at Wanstead, not even such a memory.

SOUTH WEALD

The well in the field at South Weald, near Brentwood, was once used by pilgrims and was first mentioned by Dr Allen in 1699. The vicar of South Weald wrote in 1866 that it was frequented by the sick folk of the neighbourhood and especially by the poor lepers from the hospital in Brook Street near by, on account of its healing properties. The brick-work over the well had been disfigured by visitors scratching their names and initials as tokens of their gratitude for the small mercies received or imagined.

Local workmen also used the well, but by the beginning of the twentieth century the structure itself looked neglected and the water had become dirty and uninviting.

There is now only a dip in the ground to show where one of the few chalybeate springs was sited.

FELSTED

One of the lesser wells the writers have visited is that near Felsted. Although Allen refers to it in his book as being chalybeate water Trinder wrote that the flavour was not strong and it was pure and clear like Tunbridge water. He said that people who suffered from convulsive diseases would have been recommended to drink it.

Christy said that from his researches he found that it was known about in Roman times and later by the monks of Little Dunmow Priory who had a path from the priory to the spring. The spring was, in 1910, bricked into the wall of the garden owned by Mr Hastings Warrin. When the writers found the property and asked the present owner about the spring we were shown a few pieces of curved brick-work in a boggy ditch in the garden. The present owner's parents bought the property in 1920 but there were no signs of the well at that time.

There were many more springs and wells in Essex that have been used, over the centuries, as 'cures' for many ailments, but they do not exist any more except in folk tales. Most have been covered by buildings or have been filled in for safety's sake. There are no oldest inhabitants left to show researchers where the wells were sited and how they produced miraculous results. Sometimes there is only a reference to a spring in an old estate book or a mark on an old map, but that has not prevented the writers from travelling around Essex and standing as near as possible to where the spas and mineral waters of Essex once were.

Upminster Well in 1907

Miller Christie thought this to be the site of Woodford Wells
Both drawings by H A Cole

FINAL THOUGHTS

The Mineral Waters of Essex can roughly be divided into three groups. In the first group are the three spa towns of Witham, Hockley, and Dovercourt with their pump rooms and entertainment suites. There were rooms for card games and dances at Witham and at Dovercourt there were a library and reading rooms, where books could be borrowed and newspapers and periodicals could be read. Hockley was slightly different because the building still stands in the village whilst the other two spas have vanished.

The second group consists of the wells whose water was bottled and sold. West Tilbury Hall provided a mineral water whose medical and curative properties were endorsed by doctors and physicians at London hospitals and consultants to famous people like King George II. There was also a rival supply from the Rector's Field, which was bottled and sold in London.

Vange Water was discovered in the nineteenth century and developed into a business with countrywide sales thanks to the national newspapers. However, like Tilbury Hall Water there was a rival water company called the Crystal Well Company. This rivalry led to competition with advertisements in the *Grays and Tilbury Gazette* proclaiming their virtues whilst deriding the other. Both these wells were closed by 1926.

Hockley Spa water was bottled in 1983, but the business was before the vogue of drinking bottled mineral water bought in supermarkets became popular.

The Spring Cool Water Company at Wickham Bishops began in 1996 and is still growing. The company has worldwide sales and seems to be flourishing.

Wells and springs in the third group can be said to be mainly local. Locals and their physicians used them for digestive complaints, skin rashes and eye infections. Some were named after a local saint, as at St Chad's Well. Others were discovered and written about by Dr Benjamin Allen in 1699. Some of these waters were used as domestic supplies and a few 'cured' local people. They were only short lived and had dried up by the time Miller Christy wrote his book.

Mr. Christy visited many of the wells we have written about and several of them were still used at the beginning of the twentieth century. He had water from nine wells analysed and came to the conclusion that only three of them, Upminster Hockley, and South Weald, had the qualities of mineral water and could perhaps have medical uses, Of the other six wells Felsted, Woodford, both West Tilbury Waters, Hornchurch, Stapleford Abbots and St Chad's Well were not mineral springs, despite claims by physicians that they cured ailments. Local stories and claims by people kept most of these wells going, but the arrival of piped water provided by water companies and the general well-being and personal hygiene led to their demise and today none is left, although the sites of a few are marked by plaques.

The writers feel that a spa of a different kind that was never completed needs a mention. This was the seawater spa that was planned by Robert Adam at Mistley Thorne.

Towards the end of the eighteenth century a rival to spas was appearing in the form of seaside resorts

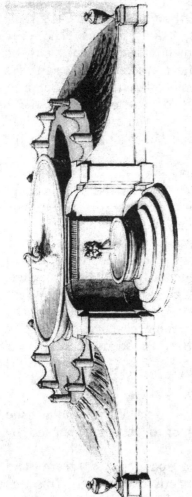

Robert Adam's design for the
Swan Lake fountain
By permission of Sir Joan
Soame's Museum

St Chad's Well, photographed
in 1910 by George E Tasker

with sea bathing facilities. These were rivalling the spring waters not only for bathing but also for drinking the water and for social activities. In Essex, Harwich, Brightlingsea and Southend were becoming the places for the aristocracy to be seen. It was planned that Mistley too would become one of these resorts.

Mistley Hall was the seat of the Right Honourable Richard Rigby, MP. Rigby and his father had built quays, houses and warehouses along the waterside. In 1770 Robert Adam was commissioned to produce a series of plans for lodges at the entrance to Mistley Park, a church and the salt-water baths. The plans included a private cold bath, a private hot bath and a public cold bath. The proposed site for them was on the quay in front of an inn. The baths were to be fed from a reservoir, itself fed from the sea. This basin is now all that remains, a round pond with a statue of a swan as a poignant reminder of the spa that never was. It can be seen at the side of the main road through Mistley

However, the fact that none of the wells and springs still exists has not made the writing about them impossible. There is plenty of documentary evidence in the Record Office and local museums. Maps and local collections in libraries have provided sources of information and it has been fun and very interesting to find where a well or spring might have been. Most are now under housing estates or dual-carriage roads.

So, the writers hope that the reader will also set out around the roads and by-ways in search of Essex spas and mineral waters.

REFERENCES

The writers wish to acknowledge the help from the following people and organisations -
Raymond Bentley, Randal Bingley, John Branch, Terry Carter, Georgina Green, Michael Guinness, Clifford Hunt, Keith Mills, Bruce Osborn, Brian Page, John Palombi, Jane Pearson, John Pirie, Raymond Pledger, Albert Poulter, Peter Pratt, Bruce Smart, Chris Strachan, Leonard Weaver, W Wilford and Mr Woodley.

Anglia Television; Basildon District Council; British Library Newspaper Library; Cambridge University Library; Dedman Property Services; Essex County Libraries: branches at Basildon, Brentwood, Chelmsford, Colchester, Dovercourt, Hockley, Loughton, Rayleigh, Witham; Essex Record Office; Guildhall Library; Harwich Town Council; Havering Libraries; Manningtree Museum; Ministry of Defence; National Monuments Record; Newsquest Essex; Redbridge Libraries; Rochford District Council; Sir John Soames Museum; Southend Museum; Southend-on-Sea Borough Libraries; Spring Cool Soft Drinks; The Wellcome Trust; Thurrock Libraries; Thurrock Museum; Vestry House Museum

BIBLIOGRAPHY

Books and Directories

Addison, William - English spas, 1951
Alderson, F - Inland resorts and spas of England
Allen, Benjamin - The Natural History of the Chalybeate and Purging Waters of England, 1699
Allen, Benjamin - The Natural History of the Mineral Waters of Great Britain, 1711
Andree, John - An Account of the Tilbury Water, 1781
Benton, Philip - The History of Rochford Hundred, 1867
Bolton, Arthur T - The Architecture of Robert and John Adam
Bramston, John - Witham in Olden Times, 1855
Brown, A F G - English History from Essex Sources 1750- 1900, ERO, 1952
Brown, A F J - Witham in the 18th Century, WEA, 1963
Burgess, Eleanor and Pearce, Mary - Boreham
Carrey, Terry - Thurrock in the 20s, Thurrock Borough Council, 1990

Christy, Miller - A History of the Mineral Waters and Medicinal
    Springs of Essex, 1911
Complete Pocket Book, 1799
Denbigh, Kathleen - A Hundred British Spas, Spa Publications,
    1981
Foord, A S - Springs, Streams and Spas of London, 1910
Granville, Augustus B - Spas of England, 1841
Havins, Peter J N - Spas of England
Hembry, Phyllis - The English Spa 1815-the Present Day, 1957
Jackson's Almanac, 1885
Jarrold's Guide to Harwich, c.1898
Jowitt, R L P and D M - Discovering Spas, Shire, 1971
Kelly's Directory.
Kent's Directory, 1779
Lewin, Joan - The English Spa, 1560-1815, Athlone Press, 1990
Lucas, Peter - Basildon - Birth of a City, 1986
Lysons, Daniel - The Environs of London, 1796
Morant, Philip - History and Antiquities of Essex, 1768
New and Complete History of Essex from a late survey, by A
    Gentleman, 1772
Noble, W F A - Survey of the Hundred of Rochford in the County
    of Essex, 1867
Payne, Jessie K - Basildon - A Pictorial History, Phillimore, 1981
Pevsner, Nikolaus - The Buildings of England - Essex, Penguin,
    1954
Phillips, Richard - A Brief Account of Hockley Spa, 1842
Phillips, Winifred V - Wanstead through the Ages, 1946
Post Office Directory
Poulter, A - In and About Witham, 1981
Searle, Muriel V - Spas and Watering Places, 1977
Smith, J - Historical Memoranda of Harwich and Dovercourt
Smith, W K J - Dovercourt and its Spa
Tasker, George E - Ilford Past and Present, 1901
Taylor, Silas and Dale, Samuel - The History and Antiquities of
    Harwich & Dovercourt, 1670
Taverner, James - An Essay upon the Witham Spa, 1711
Trinder, W Martin - Medicinal Waters in the County of Essex,
    1783
Twenty-eight views of Harwich, Dovercourt & Neighbourhood,
    Newman & Co
Universal Pocket Companion, 1745
Victoria County History of Essex

Visitor's Guide to Harwich and Dovercourt, 1864
Weaver, Leonard - Harwich - Gateway to the Continent, Dalton
White, William - History Gazetteer & Directory of the County of
    Essex, 1848/1862

Newspapers and Journals

Country Life; Essex & West Suffolk Gazette; Essex Chronicle
(Chelmsford Chronicle); Essex Countryside; Essex County
Standard; Essex County Telegraph; Essex Herald; Essex
Naturalist; Essex Review; Essex Standard (and General
Advertiser); Essex Weekly News; Evening Echo (Southend Echo);
Gazetteer and New Daily Advertiser; Grays and Tilbury Gazette;
Harwich and Dovercourt Standard; Havering History Review -
The Journal of the Hornchurch & District Historical Society;
Highlight - Journal of the Harwich Society; Independent
(Redbridge); Ipswich Journal; Morning Herald and Daily
Advertiser; Panorama - Thurrock Historical Society Journal;
(Parker's) General Advertiser & Morning Intelligencer; Romford
Record - Journal of the Romford Historical Society; Shell Haven
News; Southend Pictorial; Southend Standard (Recorder);
Southend Star; The Times; Transactions of the Essex
Archæological Society; Westminster Gazette; Witham &
Braintree Times; Witham & Countryside Society Bulletin; Yellow
Advertiser

The name of the pub is all that remains of the Woodford Wells